ROBIN - SON OF BATMAN

VOLUME 2
DAWN OF
THE DEMONS

WRITTEN BY
PATRICK GLEASON
RAY FAWKES

PENCILS BY
PATRICK GLEASON
SCOTT MCDANIEL
RAMON BACHS

INKS BY
MICK GRAY
ANDY OWENS
RAMON BACHS

COLORS BY
JOHN KALISZ
CHRIS SOTOMAYOR
MAT LOPES

LETTERS BY
TOM NAPOLITANO
COREY BREEN
DERON BENNETT

COLLECTION COVER ARTISTS
PATRICK GLEASON,
MICK GRAY & JOHN KALISZ

BATMAN CREATED BY
BOB KANE WITH BILL FINGER

MARK DOYLE Editor – Original Series
REBECCA TAYLOR Associate Editor – Original Series
JEB WOODARD Group Editor – Collected Editions
STEVE COOK Design Director – Books
DAMIAN RYLAND Publication Design

BOB HARRAS Senior VP – Editor-in-Chief, DC Comics

DIANE NELSON President
DAN DIDIO and JIM LEE Co-Publishers
GEOFF JOHNS Chief Creative Officer
AMIT DESAI Senior VP – Marketing & Global Franchise Management
NAIRI GARDINER Senior VP – Finance
SAM ADES VP – Digital Marketing
BOBBIE CHASE VP – Talent Development
MARK CHIARELLO Senior VP – Art, Design & Collected Editions
JOHN CUNNINGHAM VP – Content Strategy
ANNE DEPIES VP – Strategy Planning & Reporting
DON FALLETTI VP – Manufacturing Operations
LAWRENCE GANEM VP – Editorial Administration & Talent Relations
ALISON GILL Senior VP – Manufacturing & Operations
HANK KANALZ Senior VP – Editorial Strategy & Administration
JAY KOGAN VP – Legal Affairs
DEREK MADDALENA Senior VP – Sales & Business Development
JACK MAHAN VP – Business Affairs
DAN MIRON VP – Sales Planning & Trade Development
NICK NAPOLITANO VP – Manufacturing Administration
CAROL ROEDER VP – Marketing
EDDIE SCANNELL VP – Mass Account & Digital Sales
COURTNEY SIMMONS Senior VP – Publicity & Communications
JIM (SKI) SOKOLOWSKI VP – Comic Book Specialty & Newsstand Sales
SANDY YI Senior VP – Global Franchise Management

ROBIN – SON OF BATMAN VOLUME 2: DAWN OF THE DEMONS

DC Comics, 2900 West Alameda Ave., Burbank, CA 91505
Printed by RR Donnelley, Salem, VA, USA. 8/5/16. First Printing.
ISBN: 978-1-4012-6481-9

Library of Congress Cataloging-in-Publication Data is available.

PATRICK GLEASON plot RAY FAWKES dialogue SCOTT McDANIEL penciller ANDY OWENS inker CHRIS SOTOMAYOR colorist TOM NAPOLITANO letterer
PATRICK GLEASON, MICK GRAY & JOHN KALISZ cover

PREVIOUSLY IN ROBIN WAR...

There are amateur Robins in Gotham. In an effort to control the teen vigilante movement, Gotham's Councilwoman Athene Noctua has put laws in place that make the wearing or possessing of Robin merchandise illegal. The vigilantes were driven underground, where they were found by the real Robin—Damian Wayne—and the three men who once called themselves Robin—Dick Grayson, Jason Todd and Tim Drake. In an effort to protect the untrained Robins, Dick Grayson tipped off the Gotham police to their location, leading to the arrest of the entire group, including Damian, Jason, and Tim. Dick's intentions were to keep the children safe, but now they are fighting the elite Talons of the Court of Owls with Dick off on his own mysterious mission...

ROBIN WAR was originally published in ROBIN WAR #1 GRAYSON #15, DETECTIVE COMICS #47, WE ARE ROBIN #7, ROBIN: SON OF BATMAN #7, RED HOOD/ARSENAL #7, TEEN TITANS #15, GOTHAM ACADEMY #13 and ROBIN WAR #2.

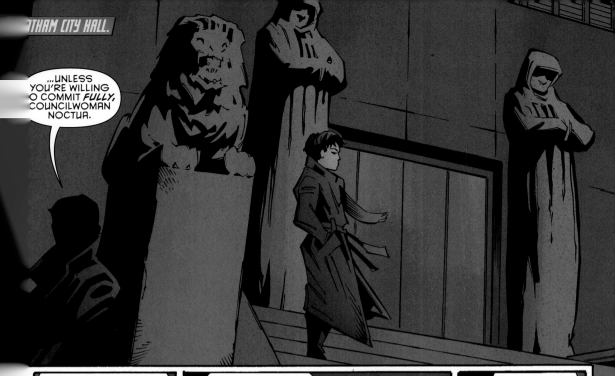

...UNLESS YOU'RE WILLING TO COMMIT *FULLY,* COUNCILWOMAN NOCTUA.

I'VE DONE *EVERYTHING* THE COURT OF OWLS HAS ASKED OF ME.

BUT THIS IS TOO *OBVIOUS.* IT'S ANOTHER STEP OUTSIDE MY PURVIEW. YOU WANT ME TO TURN THE POLICE INTO YOUR PERSONAL SECURITY FORCE...

THIS IS A CRUCIAL PART OF A *GLOBAL* PLAN.

YOU WILL POSITION THE POLICE AS ORDERED *IMMEDIATELY,* OR YOUR CONSIDERATION FOR MEMBERSHIP IN THE COURT WILL BE *WITHDRAWN...*

...ALONG WITH ITS *PROTECTION.*

...GLOBAL?

YOU HAVE *TEN* SECONDS.

GET ME JIM GORDON.

BATMAN. I'M SORRY TO BOTHER YOU. THIS IS AN *EMERGENCY.*

"I'M SERIOUS, NOW. *DEADLY* SERIOUS..."

BETTER ANGELS
PATRICK GLEASON writer & penciller   **MICK GRAY** inker   **JOHN KALISZ** colorist   **TOM NAPOLITANO** letterer   **PATRICK GLEASON, MICK GRAY & JOHN KALISZ** cover

PREVIOUSLY IN ROBIN WAR...

As the war between the Court of Owls and the Robins escalated, a seemingly evil Damian fought a pitched battle with Duke, leader of the Robin vigilante movement. Despite a severe beating from Damian, Duke convinced the son of Batman that he was the true Robin and freed him from the Owls' talons. Unbeknownst to everyone, Dick joined the Court of Owls in order to bring an end to the Robin Laws and peace to Gotham City once again.

FWUMP

FWUMP

HRHN. LAMPS. MY...BEAUTIFUL... LAMPY...

IT'S LIGHTS OUT, BATHEAD. GCPD PATROL WILL BE BY SOON TO TAKE YOU BAT-FREAKS BACK TO ARKHAM.

CURSES. JETS SPENT. FIRST THESE PESTS, NOW DRIFTING OVER THE FILTH OF THE HARBOR. I'LL NEED A STRONG DOSE OF ANTIBIOTICS AFTER THIS NIGHT IS OVER.

WHA--?

LIGHTS?... UNDER THE HARBOR BRIDGE? WHO WOULD BE--

NO. WAIT... THE BOAT?... DUCARD!

CHANK

NOBODY!

SNORF?

...BUT SHE'S HAPPY...

DEET

I KNOW, BOY...

...SHE'S SAFE.

WELL?

IF I *MUST* SUFFER THROUGH THIS, YOU MAY AS WELL GET STARTED.

WE TALKED ABOUT THIS, MASTER DAMIAN. YOU'RE WELL PAST DUE FOR A *HAIRCUT.*

YOU AGREED, ON THE CONDITION THAT WE DO IT HERE IN THE BATCAVE. SO STOP *FIDGETING.*

I DO *NOT* FIDGET.

THIS IS INTERMINABLE! WE'LL BE HERE ALL NIGHT! AND NOT SO SHORT!

CAN'T I DO IT *MYSELF?*

≶SIGH≶

SNIP SNIP

PERHAPS THE TIME WILL GO QUICKER IF YOU TELL ME A TALE.

AT DINNER YOU MADE AN INTERESTING ALLUSION TO A... WHAT WAS IT? A "CUTLESS CUTLASS"?

THE *BLOODLESS BLADE.*

I *SHOULD* TELL YOU ABOUT THAT. I ALMOST DIED *AGAIN,* AFTER ALL...

...ONLY *THIS* TIME...

THE YEAR OF BLOOD. DAY 202.

"...I DON'T KNOW IF YOU CAN *HANDLE* IT IN THERE..."

"EVEN THE *ELITE FOOTMEN* OF THE LEAGUE OF ASSASSINS, WHO DO NOT HAVE THE *CAPACITY* FOR MORTAL FEAR..."

"...EVEN THEY WERE *NOT IMMUNE*..."

"...WHO LEARN *ABSOLUTE* CONTROL OVER THEIR *HEARTS* AND *MINDS*..."

"...AND COULD NOT SURVIVE WHAT *I* ENDURED."

AAAGH! LIKE... ICE...

NUH-NO.

I AM ~~D~~AMIAN AL ~~GH~~UL.

I AM NO ORDINARY *SOUL.* YOU *CANNOT* KILL ME WITH YOUR GHOST MAGIC. YOUR "BLOODLESS BLADE."

NOTHING CAN STOP ME.

⸔GASP⸕

SO WHAT, YOU HAD TO FIGHT A SACRED IMMORTAL KUNG FU DUDE? OOH, *SCARY*.

YOU KNOW I'M GOING IN WITH YOU NO MATTER *WHAT* YOU SAY, RIGHT? I CAN TOTALLY HANDLE ANYTHING YOU CAN.

I DIDN'T FIGHT HIM...

HRRF.

"...THOUGH I DID FACE HIS *HEROIC WRATH*, AND I TOOK HIS *LEGENDARY WEAPON* FROM HIM."

SO LET'S GO. I'M SURE HE'LL BE *HAPPY* TO HAVE HIS FANCY SPEAR BACK.

YOU CAN GET YOUR *ATONE-MENT* DONE AND WE CAN GET OUT OF THIS *DEEP FREEZE*.

LAST WARNING...

"...YOU MAY *REGRET* THIS."

‹HEED THIS WARNING, THIEF.›

‹YOU HAVE *GIVEN* AND YOU HAVE *TAKEN*. AND WHEN YOU RETURN TO THIS PLACE, FOR *RETURN* YOU WILL...›

"(...YOU, AT YOUR VERY *WORST*, WILL TAKE AND GIVE *TWICE AS MUCH*...)"

UGH, IT'S EVEN *COLDER* IN *HERE*.

I THOUGHT ONCE WE WERE OUT OF THAT *SHRIEKING WIND*...

SHH. SOMETHING'S *DIFFERENT*.

SO WHY DID YOU HAVE TO STEAL THIS *SPEAR*, ANYWAY?

WAS IT, LIKE, *FATED* TO GIVE YOUR GRAND-FATHER *UNTOLD POWER* LIKE EVERYTHING ELSE APPARENTLY IS?

WILL YOU BE *QUIET*?

"I'M RA'S AL GHUL, AND WITH THIS COCKTAIL NAPKIN OF GLORY, I SHALL FINALLY *RULE*--"

IF YOU *MUST* KNOW, THE SPEAR WAS ONLY THE *PROOF* THAT I CONQUERED UNUTTERABLE *FEAR* AND SURVIVED THIS *TRIAL*.

WAIT, WHAT'S THAT *SNOW* DOING?

SSSSSHH--

BUT WE WILL *NOT* BECOME YOU.

OH NO, NOT *MORE* OF THIS--

NO, LOOK.

WE HAVE THEIR *RESPECT*.

IT'S NOT AN EASY THING, WHAT WE JUST DID.

YEAH. HEY, SO, WHAT YOU SAID? ABOUT HOW YOU'LL NEVER BECOME THAT NASTY?

PLEASE *DON'T*, OKAY?

I SHOULD SAY THE SAME TO YOU.

...ACTUALLY FEELS A LITTLE BIT *WARMER* OUT HERE IN THIS COZY *BLIZZARD*.

NOW WHERE DID *GOLIATH* GET TO?

FWEEEEEE

...IT WON'T COME *BACK.*

SO LET ME GUESS. NEXT UP: YOU NEED TO ATONE FOR, LIKE, NOT *RELAXING* ENOUGH ON A NICE, *WARM* LEGENDARY BEACH SOME-WHERE?

TELL ME I'M RIGHT.

"AND LET ME TELL *YOU,* ALFRED. IF I HAVE MY WAY..."

SNIP
SNIP

...I'LL BE HAPPY IF I NEVER SEE ANOTHER *PRETENTIOUS* OLD TEMPLE LIKE THAT AGAIN.

INDEED?

HMM. BUT IT SOUNDS LIKE THE EXPERIENCE WAS...*ENLIGHTENING?*

⋝TT⋜

I SUPPOSE YOU COULD CALL IT THAT.

WELL, YOU'RE DONE, AT ANY RATE.

GOOD AS NEW.

AM I?

WELL, WITH THE HAIRCUT.

AH. YES.

YOU UNDERSTAND I'M NOT DONE WITH THE *ATONEMENT*, ALFRED.

SO MUCH OF WHAT I DID IN THE YEAR OF BLOOD MUST BE *CORRECTED*. I WENT *FAR* DOWN THE PATH MY MOTHER LAID OUT.

I DO *NOT* WANT TO BECOME THE MAN SHE ENVISIONED.

YES, MASTER DAMIAN.

I UNDERSTAND PERFECTLY. WILL YOU TAKE YOUR DINNER DOWN *HERE*, OR *UPSTAIRS?*

WRAP IT FOR ME.

I'LL EAT IT ON THE *ROAD.*

IM... IMPOSSIBLE

I...*FAILED*...

I DO NOT *UNDERSTAND*...

THE LU'UN DARGA *MUST* RETURN. OUR DESTINY...TO DEFEAT THE AL GHUL FAMILY... TO EXTINGUISH *ALL* LIFE...

THE *ARTIFACTS* THE AL GHUL CHILD RETURNED SHOULD HAVE GIVEN ME THE POWER I NEEDED...

TO BRING YOU...TO BRING YOU ALL *BACK* TO--

SHHH...

ONE OF US WILL BE QUITE ENOUGH...

...*FATHER*...

"...LET HER LIVE *THIS* LAST DAY IN PLACE."

WHAT THE--

NO...

SNFF
SNFF

SNORF!

I KNOW, GOLIATH.

KRANG

THE ENEMY IS HERE!

IN THE NAME OF THE LU'UN DARGA, YOU ARE SENTENCED...

I DON'T HAVE TO ASK IF YOU *KNOW* WHAT YOU'VE DONE.

YOU KNOW *PERFECTLY* WELL.

HSSSSSS

COME, GOLIATH.

THE ANTI-SAINT HAS HIS *SERPENT HEART* BACK NOW! HIS RAGE AT LOSING IT WILL *QUADRUPLE* THE POWER OF ITS PROTECTION!

REEYOWW!!

AIIEEE!

I HAVE NO IDEA HOW THE LU'UN DARGA MANAGED TO STEAL THESE ITEMS FROM RIGHT UNDER MY NOSE...

...BUT WE HAVEN'T *TIME* TO WORRY OVER THAT. MY SUSPICIONS ARE CONFIRMED. THEY ARE WORKING TO RETURN THEM, AND THEY'LL WILLINGLY *DIE* TO DOOM US *ALL*.

QUICKLY NOW...

MY **SHIP.** YOU'LL BE QUITE **COMFORTABLE**...IF YOU'RE TELLING THE TRUTH...

...AND IF I'M NOT SATISFIED YOU **ARE,** IT'S YOUR LAST STOP IN THIS LIFE.

NO! LET ME **GO!**

WAIT! WAIT!

IT WASN'T **ME,** I **SWEAR!** WHAT'S **HAPPENING?**

YOU WILL SPEAK WHEN **SPOKEN** TO!

AND YOUR DENIALS MEAN NOTHING TO ME UNTIL YOU CAN **EXPLAIN...**

OUR AGENT IN **CHIHUAHUA** HAS **PERISHED,** LADY **TALIA.**

HIS LAST MESSAGE WAS **INCOMPLETE.**

SET A COURSE FOR THE **SECOND** TARGET.

OUT OF MY WAY, *PEON!*

CLEAR THE *PATH!*

THIS IS BETWEEN *ME*--

THOK

Hnnf!

Aargh!

THOK

--AND THE FIRE BOY--

Nnnah!

NONE STAY THE HAND OF THE LU'UN DARGA!

NOW, *DIE!*

GET OFF ME!

PSSSHT

LU'UN DARGA *FANATICS!*

THOK

WHA

DON'T YOU REALIZE YOU'LL *ALL* DIE, TOO? WHEN HE COMPLETES HIS *PLAN?*

DON'T YOU REALIZE I'M THE ONLY HOPE YOU *HAVE?!*

BRUKK

WELL, WELL. AT LEAST YOU'RE AS TOUGH TO KILL AS *ANY* AL GHUL.

I WAS FEELING A LITTLE DISAPPOINTED, THINKING I'D *DESTROYED* YOU WITHIN SECONDS OF OUR FIRST MEETING...

WHY! WHY WOULD YOU *BRING* HER HERE?

SHE WAS *HAPPY!*

SHE WAS A *LU'UN DARGA* SPY, DAMIAN. SHE LED THEM TO YOUR VAULT.

IMPOSSIBLE! MAYA WOULD *NEVER* TURN ON ME! SHE FOUGHT AT YOUR SIDE!

BUT... DAMIAN...

HOW *DARE* YOU, MOTHER!

NEVER SPEAK THAT WAY ABOUT HER AGAIN!

YOU'RE *HURT.* LET ME HAVE A LOOK.

≥TT≤

THERE'S NO TIME TO *LOSE,* FATHER.

IF MOTHER IS RIGHT, WE CAN STILL STOP THE SON OF DARGA, BUT WE MUST *COOPERATE.*

MOTHER... FATHER...

WILL YOU WORK SIDE BY SIDE WITHOUT FIGHTING EACH *OTHER?*

WILL YOU *JOIN* ME?

TO SAVE THE WORLD, MY SON.

ONLY TO SAVE THE **WORLD.**

LIKE YOU SAID, DAMIAN. NO TIME TO WASTE. I DIDN'T MANAGE TO GET A TRACKER ON HIM, BUT MAYBE YOUR FRIEND MAYA--

I **KNOW** WHERE HE'S GOING.

THERE IS ONE **LAST** ITEM MISSING FROM THE VAULT. THE MOST POWERFUL ONE I KEPT FROM THE YEAR OF BLOOD.

THE MOST DIFFICULT TO **STEAL** AND THE MOST DIFFICULT TO **REPLACE.**

I **KNEW** HE'D SAVE IT FOR LAST. I DIDN'T EVEN WANT TO **MENTION** IT...

I'LL STOP YOU!

RRRAGH!

YOU'RE AS IRRITATING AS YOUR FRIEND DAMIAN! ARE YOU SURE YOU'RE NOT AN AL GHUL?

Aaaigh! WILL YOU JUST...HIT THE DECK ALREADY...?

Gggkk... Neh...

NEVER!

THWOCK

Owww!

⇥cough cough⇤

MY LORD.

ALL IS PREPARED FOR YOUR ARRIVAL.

WHEN THE MOON RISES INTO POSITION--

--THE RITUAL OF YOUR FATHER, DEN DARGA, WILL BE READY...

THAT WILL BE SIX HOURS FROM NOW. OUR VICTORY IS AT HAND. THE WORLD DIES AT MIDNIGHT.

YES, MY LORD.

STRANGE. I *IMMUNIZED* HER TO LU'UN DARGA TOXINS ON MY SHIP, AS A PRECAUTION. THEY MAKE CHEMICAL WEAPONS OF THEIR ALLIES SOMETIMES.

SHE SHOULDN'T BE *DEAD*.

I'M *NOT* DEAD, TALIA. SO YEAH, THANKS FOR THAT.

DON'T TOUCH ME, THOUGH. ~cough~

THEY *THOUGHT* I WAS, AND THEY *RIGGED* MY BODY. THERE'S A ~cough~ *BOMB* UNDER ME.

I KINDA DON'T KNOW WHAT TO DO.

LU'UN DARGA SCUM!

FATHER. CAN WE--

I CAN *DISARM* IT, YES. BUT IT'LL TAKE A FEW MINUTES.

GO.

WE DON'T HAVE TIME TO WAIT!

MOTHER AND I WILL GO TO *BATTLE*. JOIN US AS SOON AS YOU CAN.

DAMIAN.

BE *CAREFUL*...

QUICKLY, GOLIATH!

SKRANG!

GRRR--

RRRRAAAA!

RIDICULOUS!

BOOOOM

Hahaha!

AND NOW...

I WILL INTERROGATE SUREN DARGA AND MAKE SURE HE CAN DO NO MORE HARM.

TALIA...

DON'T WORRY, DETECTIVE. HE DOES NOT NEED TO *DIE*.

HE'LL JUST BE KEPT CUT OFF FROM THE MAGIC OF HIS *KIND* SO THAT HE CAN'T DO ANYTHING LIKE THIS AGAIN.

AS FOR YOU, MY SON.

YOU DID VERY WELL. AND YOU *ARE* AN AL GHUL, NO MATTER WHAT YOU SAY. AS *RUTHLESS* AS YOU ARE *RESOURCEFUL*.

AND I AM *VERY* PROUD OF YOU.

NOW, I MUST SPEAK WITH YOUR *FATHER* FOR A MOMENT.

HEY...

...THAT STUFF YOU SAID TO SUREN...ABOUT FEELING *ALONE* AND *UNLOVED* AND STUFF... ABOUT LOOKING FOR YOUR FATHER'S *APPROVAL*...

I MEAN, ARE YOU... *OKAY?*

WHAT? DON'T BE RIDICULOUS. I HAVE TO *TELL* YOU SOMETHING...

...HOW MUCH MORE ARE WE EXPECTED TO *DO?* I AM ABOUT TO *BURST.*

IT'S CALLED *DESSERT,* SUREN.

YOU'VE NEVER HAD DESSERT BEFORE?

I'M NOT... SURE...

...MY FATHER FORBADE INDULGENCE IN MORTAL *POISONS.* NO WONDER YOU'RE ALL TRAITORS AND COWARDS.

YOUR FATHER IS *DEN DARGA,* THE MANIAC WHO WISHES TO EXTERMINATE ALL LIFE.

MAYBE IF HE TRIED A LITTLE *BUTTERSCOTCH RIPPLE,* HE'D BE CALMER.

MAN, YOU GUYS HAVE SO MUCH IN *COMMON.*

SNORF

I BET AN *AL GHUL* FAMILY PICNIC IS JUST AS MUCH FUN AS A *DARGA* ONE.

IT'S WORSE THAN YOU CAN POSSIBLY IMAGINE, MAYA.

BE GLAD MY FATHER ARGUED THAT WE SHOULD ESCORT SUREN TO GOTHAM *BEFORE* THE WEEKEND FEAST. NOTICE HE *ALSO* CHOSE TO LEAVE FOR HIS WATCHTOWER IMMEDIATELY.

BUT NOT BEFORE SHE *TORTURED* ME.

OH, STOP WHINING. ALL SHE DID WAS SIT YOU DOWN AND ASK YOU QUESTIONS. THE TORTURE HADN'T BEGUN. SHE HAS THESE SUBMARINE *BATTERIES* ON HER SHIP, THEY--

SNNF SNNF

REEEEUUNK!

THE LU'UN DARGA HAVE FOUND US *AGAIN!*

WHAT ARE THERE, LIKE, *TEN MILLION* OF THESE GUYS?

YOUR DAD MUST'VE OFFERED SOME KINDA SWEET NINJA SIGNING BONUS, SUREN, OR—

THEY ARE FANATICS! RELEASE ME SO I CAN *DESTROY* THEM!

THEY DON'T UNDERSTAND THE BATTLE IS ALREADY *OVER.* THEY'LL KEEP COMING AFTER US UNTIL THEY KILL US...

...MEeeee.

ROBIN! THERE'S SOME KINDA *ENERGY* DRAIN...

HERE. FREQUENCY DISRUPTER! THAT'LL KEEP HIM WITH US FOR NOW. CAN YOU CALL FOR HELP? YOUR DAD OR SOMEONE?

SLAP

MY COMMS ARE OFFLINE.

THIS IS *DARGA* SPIRIT MAGIC! ONE OF SUREN'S FAMILY IS STILL *ACTIVE* SOMEWHERE. HE WAS WRONG. THIS BATTLE ISN'T OVER YET.

NOT "SOMEWHERE." I CAN *SEE* WHERE IT'S GOING. MY HELMET'S SENSORS ARE PRETTY GOOD WITH INVISIBLE ENERGY.

THEN LET'S GO...

THEY'RE ALL BEING DRAINED! WHATEVER THIS IS, IT SEEMS TO TARGET ONLY THE LU'UN DARGA!

BUT BE *CAREFUL!* WE DON'T KNOW WHAT THEIR ENERGY IS *FEEDING!*

WE OUGHT TO—

→Hoough!←

BLANGG

→Agh!←

GOLIATH...

...TAKE ME THERE...

→Tk←
I THOUGHT YOUR HELMET WAS GOOD WITH *INVISIBLE* ENERGY.

NOBODY'S *PERFECT.*

I THOUGHT YOU'RE SUPPOSED TO *BE* NOBODY.

OH, HA, HA.

WAIT, GOLIATH! DON'T--

YOU YET LIVE!

YES...

SUREN! DON'T LET HIM TOUCH YOU!

THUNK THUNK THUNK

>Hrrrgh!<

THIS SPIRIT BATTERY IS MY *CONTINGENCY.* PREPARED MILLENNIA AGO, TO BE REALIZED ONLY IF THE PROPER LU'UN DARGA APOCALYPSE WAS *THWARTED.*

THAT IT HAS ACTIVATED WHILE YOU ARE STILL *ALIVE* DEMONSTRATES YOUR *FAILURE. YOUR WEAKNESS...*

...THAT YOU WOULD LET YOURSELF *LIVE* AFTER FAILING ME DEMONSTRATES YOUR *COWARDICE* AND *INCOMPETENCE.*

FILTH. DID YOU LEARN *NOTHING* AT MY SIDE?

FATHER... YOU *LIED* TO US.

OUR SOULS WILL NOT LIVE ON IN THE NEW WORLD, WILL THEY? THEY JUST EMPOWER YOUR MAGIC. *YOU* WILL REMAIN.

YES!

ONLY I AM WORTHY! I WILL *SCOUR* THIS WORLD AND BE THE CUSTODIAN AND CREATOR OF *ALL* NEW LIFE!

NICE. HOLD STILL, LEMME SHOW YOU WHAT YOU'RE *WORTHY* OF...

YOU WERE MERELY A WEAPON TO BRING IT ABOUT WHILE I *SLEPT.*

AND NOW TO *FINISH* THIS...

POUR IT *ON!*

DON'T STOP!

YEAH!

KEEP IT GOING!

WE *GOT* THIS!

NICE ONE!

SOONER OR LATER...

...HE'LL FALL!

Hhah... hehhh...

IT DOESN'T... MATTER. I CAN...FALL...

YOU'RE *ALL* DEAD...

HE'S RIGHT. THE POWER GOING INTO THAT THING, IT'S *INSANE!*

IT'S NOT SLOWING DOWN AT ALL!

HEH... HAH...

MY BODY CAN *FAIL.* THIS SPELL WILL COMPLETE ITSELF REGARDLESS.

THE TRUE VICTORY OF DEN DARGA IS AT *HAND.* ALL YOUR *HOPES,* ALL YOUR *STRUGGLE...*

...IT WILL ALL MEAN *NOTHING.*

WHAT DO WE *DO?*

ROBIN? WHAT DO WE DO?

→TĿ←

HE *TOLD* US.

IT'S A *BATTERY*. SUREN. DID YOU LEARN TO *PULL* SPIRITS LIKE YOUR FATHER CAN? *STEER* THEM?

A... LITTLE...

CRACK

GOOD.

WHAK

DO IT NOW! GUIDE THEM ALONG THESE *WIRES*!

WE CAN SHORT IT OUT!

THE DISCHARGE... WILL *KILL* YOU, AL GHUL.

AND I WILL *REMAIN* TO DESTROY YOUR FRIENDS AND BUILD MY SPELL ANEW. EVEN IF IT TAKES *CENTURIES*...

I ENDURED THE *YEAR OF BLOOD* AND TAUGHT THE *AL GHULS* THAT I AM WORTHY TO *RULE* THIS WORLD, DEN DARGA.

AND THEN THROUGH THE *YEAR OF ATONEMENT*, I TAUGHT MYSELF THAT I AM WORTHY TO *FREE* IT FROM THE LIKES OF YOU *AND* THE AL GHULS.

NO!

THERE'S *GOT* TO BE ANOTHER WAY!

GOLIATH! ANYONE WHO TOUCHES ME... WILL CARRY THE SHOCK, TOO... STOP MAYA...

GO!

REEEEEUUNKK!

-:Hnnf!:-

KKKKKTTTTTKKKTT...

HE...HE *DID* IT...

DO YOU FEEL IT? IT'S STOPPED.

YEAH, BUT...

...HE'S *DEAD.*

REEE?

NO. NO, DAMIAN, NO...

IT'S NOT FAIR, IT'S NOT *RIGHT...*

YOU SAVED THE *WORLD.* MORE THAN *ONCE.*

BUT YOU DON'T--

WAIT. WHAT'S THAT?

WE STILL HAVE TO DO ALL KINDS OF STUFF...

...WE STILL HAVE TO FINISH THAT ICE CREAM.

~Tt~ IT WASN'T *THAT* GOOD.

DAMIAN!

WELL...IT LOOKS LIKE WE SUCCEEDED. DEN DARGA IS FINISHED.

WELL DONE, EVERYONE.

OH FOR--

HEY, MAYBE YOU COULD SAY *THANK YOU* OR SOMETHING? WE ONLY JUST PULLED YOU BACK FROM LITERAL *DEATH* WITH OUR SINCERE HEARTS OR WHATEVER...

...NO BIG *DEAL.*

YES, AS I SAID.

WELL DONE.

≥kktt≤ ROBIN. ROBIN, COME IN.

YES, BATMAN, I CAN HEAR YOU. MY COMMS ARE BACK.

ROBIN, YOU'RE THREE HOURS LATE--

DAMIAN, THIS IS YOUR MOTHER--

--WHERE ARE YOU? BRING THE DARGA BOY BACK THIS INSTANT!

≥Tt≤

--IS EVERYTHING ALL RIGHT? I CAN PICK YOU UP IF YOU NEED A RIDE.

DAMIAN, I THOUGHT WE HAD AN UNDERSTANDING. YOU--

THANK YOU, TALIA. THANK YOU, FATHER. I'M FINE!

KLIK

WELL?

WHAT ARE YOU ALL WAITING FOR?

ADVENTURE AWAITS...

ROBIN: SON OF BATMAN #8
ADULT COLORING BOOK VARIANT COVER
BY SANFORD GREENE